PRAISE FOR *O COME, EMMANUEL*

"'Truly wonderful,' St. John Chrysostom wrote, 'is the whole chronicle of the Nativity.' Kendra Tierney makes it even more wonderful by providing a scriptural map to guide the whole family to Christmas. I can't think of a better way to prepare children—and their parents—for the birth of Our Lord."

Scott Hahn
Founder and President, St. Paul Center

"O Come, Emmanuel provides for families a simple and beautiful way to live more fully the season of Advent so that we might receive Our Lord anew at Christmas. The reflections are engaging for children of all ages, and profound enough to give meat to meditation for grown-ups. This is a treasure."

Noelle Mering
Author of Theology of Home

"What a gift this book is to stressed-out moms and busy families! Advent is a season of 'too much' for many of us, but these reflections offer a gentle

antidote with a focus on Scripture and family prayer. Whether you are new to Jesse Tree devotions or a seasoned veteran of liturgical living, this book will be a simple guide to the kind of peace you are craving."

Danielle Bean
Author, Speaker, and Brand Manager of CatholicMom.com

"The holiday season can be chaotic and overwhelming. By combining Scripture, our rich Catholic tradition, and thoughtful reflections for today's families, this delightful little book will help you and your household to quiet the noise that so often accompanies the days leading up to Christmas so that you will be spiritually prepared to celebrate the birth of our Savior."

Fr. Matthew Spencer, O.S.J.
Provincial Superior, Oblates of St. Joseph

"For years, Kendra Tierney has been working tirelessly to strengthen the domestic Church by reviving Catholic traditions and celebrating the liturgical year. My family has benefitted from her

efforts, and that's why we were excited about her new book, O Come, Emmanuel. This beautifully illustrated book is simple yet profound. Each page is rich with Scripture and accompanied by meditations that are compelling to both children and the child in each of us! The Advent and Christmas seasons are my favorite times of year, and this book will be a wonderful addition for our family's celebration."

Sam Guzman
Author of The Catholic Gentleman

"Kendra delivers another great Catholic resource for the Advent season. This book allows families to prepare their homes and their hearts for the celebration of Christmas."

Kristin Reilly
Blogger, OneHailMaryAtATime.com

"As the world tries to make Christmas a secular holiday, it's important to witness within the Catholic family that we do it differently. The season of Advent is a marked and beautiful difference, a delicious appetizer before the feast of Christmas. Kendra's straightforward approach to the Jesse Tree

beautifully combines the practical and profound. With well-chosen Scripture passages, Old Testament symbology, and a busy-family formula, the entire family is swept through the adventurous and extravagant love story of salvation."

Hope Schneir
Songwriter and Mother of Nine

O COME, EMMANUEL

O COME, EMMANUEL

ADVENT REFLECTIONS ON
THE JESSE TREE FOR FAMILIES

Kendra Tierney
Illustrated by Peggy Pilapil-Lasa

EMMAUS
ROAD
PUBLISHING

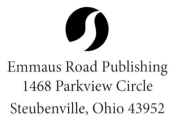

Emmaus Road Publishing
1468 Parkview Circle
Steubenville, Ohio 43952

Library of Congress Control Number: 2020945784
978-1-64585-076-2 hardcover | 978-1-64585-077-9 ebook

Cover design and layout by Patty Borgman

DEDICATION:

To my nieces Lucy, Emma, and Skylar and to my nephews Jude, Vinnie, Luke, Brendon, Mike, and Sean. May you always wait in wonder and grow in love.

ACKNOWLEDGEMENTS:

With grateful thanks to Grace Brown, Abbey Davis Dupuy, and Jeff Gottesfeld for sharing your unique perspectives and good advice.

TABLE OF CONTENTS

INTRODUCTION

I LOVE ADVENT. There's something about this season of anticipation and preparation that draws me in each year. Many of our family's favorite liturgical living traditions are tied to Advent, so I was really excited when the good folks at Emmaus Road Publishing asked me to be a part of this project.

The Jesse Tree is an Advent devotion that invites us to prepare for the birth of Jesus by tracing salvation history through the study of scripture and Christian symbols. In this book, we'll look closely at details of a lovely illustration, and at details from stories in the Bible, and we'll see them come together to present a complete picture of the Nativity of Jesus.

In theory, Advent is a season of quiet and waiting. In practice it can be hectic and busy and stressful, and/or overlooked entirely as we rush right past it to begin celebrating Christmas. Creating prayerful family traditions is a great way to foster the spirit of hopeful anticipation proper to Advent.

There are different practices associated with the Jesse Tree as it is observed by different families.

Reading the book together each day is the heart of the devotion. By becoming familiar with these heroes and villains and regular folks of the Bible, we can see how their stories and symbols entwine across thousands of years to prepare humanity for the coming of the Redeemer. Any time in the day that we can grab a few moments with the family and this book—be it over a meal or in the car or cuddled on the couch in front of a fire—is going to emphasize the true meaning of Advent and Christmas, and help encourage our family's growth in faith and understanding.

In our home, we like best to gather together in the evening, after dinner and before the youngest kids go to bed. Different members of the family take turns reading on different nights. It only takes a few minutes . . . and, importantly, we don't sweat the pronunciation of proper names too much.

We are a big family with kids that range from infant to young adult. Family prayer time is a priority. We emphasize its importance by asking grownups and older kids to plan around it whenever possible, and, when that's not possible, by moving it to a time of day when we'll catch the most people. Friends and neighbors are always welcome to join us!

Often, the Bible stories we read lead to conversations and questions. Sometimes, we grownups don't know the answers to those questions off the tops of our heads. But it's always okay to say, "I don't know, but I'll find out." We can look into it, then come back to that question the next day. No matter how problematic an issue might seem, I've always found that saints and scholars have had the same questions before we have, and have come up with comforting and consistent answers to them.

If we're looking to level up a bit, we'll also hang an ornament each day after we finish the readings. Some families hang them on a large bare branch leaned against a wall or secured in a pot of sand or rocks. Others put up a Christmas tree early, but hold off on decorating it during Advent, using it to hang Jesse Tree ornaments instead. Our family waits to put up our tree until Christmas Eve. After we read each day's section from the book, we hang a small ornament on a decorative fabric wall-hanging tree intended to be an Advent calendar.

If we have the time, reading a seasonal picture book or chapter book, and/or singing an Advent-appropriate carol or two, then rolling right into bedtime prayers is a lovely way to end the devotion.

Sometimes life happens and we miss a day. In that case, we'll usually just make it up by doing two the next day. If for some reason we got many days behind, I'd probably just jump ahead to the current day, hang up as many ornaments as we needed to catch up, and figure I'd try to get all of the readings in the next year.

Like all liturgical living, like life itself, it's not about being perfect. It's about spending time with family and scripture, and growing together in knowledge, understanding, faith, and personal holiness. If you're interested in learning more about liturgical living traditions for all year long, look me up online or come find me on social media. My prayer is that this book will help make your family's Advent a little more holy and your Christmas a little more joyous.

MAY GOD BLESS US, EVERY ONE!
Kendra Tierney, 2020

A STUMP FROM THE TREE OF JESSE

ISAIAH 11:1–5, 10

There shall come forth a shoot from the stump of
Jesse,
    and a branch shall grow out of his roots.
And the Spirit of the Lord shall rest upon him,
    the spirit of wisdom and understanding,
    the spirit of counsel and might,
    the spirit of knowledge and the fear of the Lord.
And his delight shall be in the fear of the Lord.

He shall not judge by what his eyes see,
    or decide by what his ears hear;
but with righteousness he shall judge the poor,
    and decide with equity for the meek of the earth;
and he shall strike the earth with the rod of his
mouth,
    and with the breath of his lips he shall slay the
wicked.
Righteousness shall be the belt of his waist,
    and faithfulness the belt of his loins. . . .

In that day the root of Jesse shall stand as an
ensign to the peoples; him shall the nations seek,
and his dwellings shall be glorious.

TODAY WE SEE A STUMP FROM WHICH A GREEN SHOOT GROWS. We read Isaiah's prophecy concerning Jesse, the father of King David. Medieval artistic representations of the Jesse Tree feature a sleeping Jesse with Jesus's family tree growing out of his torso. On each branch is one of Christ's ancestors, and at the top is the Virgin Mary holding the child Jesus. These pictures remind us that although Jesus is God, and the son of God, he is also a man, descended from Mary, and before that David, and Jesse, and all the way back to our first parents, Adam and Eve.

As Christians, each of us is also part of this family tree! Jesus tells us, "I am the vine, you are the branches" (Jn 15:5). We are branches reaching out to share the light and love of Jesus with our family, our friends, and the world.

O God, we love you as true God and true man. Help us to prepare our homes for the celebration of Christmas and our hearts for the Incarnation. AMEN.

GOD'S CREATION

GENESIS 1:1, 3, 5–6, 8–10, 13–15, 18–21, 23–24, 26–27, 31; 2:1, 3

In the beginning God created the heavens and the earth.

And God said, "Let there be light"; and there was light. God called the light Day, and the darkness he called Night. And there was evening and there was morning, one day.

And God said, "Let there be a firmament in the midst of the waters, and let it separate the waters from the waters. And God called the firmament Heaven. And there was evening and there was morning, a second day.

And God said, "Let the waters under the heavens be gathered together into one place, and let the dry land appear." . . . God called the dry land Earth, and the waters that were gathered together he called Seas. And God saw that it was good. And there was evening and there was morning, a third day.

And God said, "Let there be lights in the firmament of the heavens to separate the day from the night; and let them be for signs and for seasons and for days and years, and let them be lights in the firmament

of the heavens to give light upon the earth." And God saw that it was good. And there was evening and there was morning, a fourth day.

And God said, "Let the waters bring forth swarms of living creatures, and let birds fly above the earth across the firmament of the heavens." So God created the great sea monsters and every living creature that moves, with which the waters swarm, according to their kinds, and every winged bird according to its kind. And God saw that it was good. And there was evening and there was morning, a fifth day.

And God said, "Let the earth bring forth living creatures according to their kinds: cattle and creeping things and beasts of the earth according to their kinds." And it was so.

Then God said, "Let us make man in our image, after our likeness; and let them have dominion over the fish of the sea, and over the birds of the air, and over the cattle, and over all the earth, and over every creeping thing that creeps upon the earth." So God created man in his own image, in the image of God he created him; male and female he created them. . . . And God saw everything that he had made, and behold, it was very good. And

there was evening and there was morning, a sixth day.

Thus the heavens and the earth were finished, and all the host of them. So God blessed the seventh day and hallowed it, because on it God rested from all his work which he had done in creation.

TODAY WE SEE THE LAND AND THE SKY AND THE TREE, AND WE READ ABOUT THE SIX DAYS OF CREATION IN GENESIS. We are reminded that God created the whole world—the whole universe—and everything in it. The beauty of the sky, the vastness of the ocean, the multitude of the creatures, all shout out the glory of God. Each twinkling star in the night sky, each shimmering fish darting through the water, each blade of grass was brought into being through God's love. He looked at all of it and called it good.

God created us in his image and likeness. Like God, we have the true freedom to understand and choose and love what is good. We are capable of knowing and loving one another. We can recognize our responsibility to care for God's creation: our world and the people in it.

O God, you said, "Let there be light." Help us to see the lights we'll use to decorate our houses and Christmas trees as a symbol of the love you have for your creation. Help us to be a light in the world, showing your love to others. AMEN.

14

THE FIRST SIN

GENESIS 3:1-13

Now the serpent was more subtle than any other wild creature that the Lord God had made. He said to the woman, "Did God say, 'You shall not eat of any tree of the garden'?" And the woman said to the serpent, "We may eat of the fruit of the trees of the garden; but God said, 'You shall not eat of the fruit of the tree which is in the midst of the garden, neither shall you touch it, lest you die.' "

But the serpent said to the woman, "You will not die. For God knows that when you eat of it your eyes will be opened, and you will be like God, knowing good and evil." So when the woman saw that the tree was good for food, and that it was a delight to the eyes, and that the tree was to be desired to make one wise, she took of its fruit and ate; and she also gave some to her husband, and he ate. Then the eyes of both were opened, and they knew that they were naked; and they sewed fig leaves together and made themselves aprons.

And they heard the sound of the Lord God walking in the garden in the cool of the day, and the man and his wife hid themselves from the presence of the Lord God among the trees of the garden. But

the Lord God called to the man, and said to him, "Where are you?"

And he said, "I heard the sound of you in the garden, and I was afraid, because I was naked; and I hid myself." He said, "Who told you that you were naked? Have you eaten of the tree of which I commanded you not to eat?" The man said, "The woman whom you gave to be with me, she gave me fruit of the tree, and I ate." Then the Lord God said to the woman, "What is this that you have done?" The woman said, "The serpent beguiled me, and I ate."

TODAY WE SEE THE FORBIDDEN FRUIT AND READ ABOUT OUR FIRST PARENTS. God wanted Adam and Eve to be able to choose love and obedience in a meaningful way, but true obedience can't exist without the possibility of disobedience. He put into the garden that one tree, and gave them that one rule. But the devil tempted Eve and, through her, Adam, and they ate the forbidden fruit and sin was brought into the world.

We call this Original Sin because it was the first sin ever committed by man. When they disobeyed God, Adam and Eve lost the gift of God's grace that

protected them from suffering and death. They could no longer pass this grace on to their children, or to their children's children, or to us. Through disobedience the gates of heaven were barred, but through obedience they were reopened. For this reason we call Jesus the new Adam, and his mother Mary the new Eve.

O God, we are born lacking the fullness of grace that you desired for us. We thank you for the gift of Baptism, through which we are restored. We hope for eternal life with you in heaven. AMEN.

THE GREAT FLOOD

GENESIS 6:11, 13-14, 17-18, 22; 7:1-5, 17; 8:1, 10-11, 20;
9:12-13

Now the earth was corrupt in God's sight, and the earth was filled with violence. . . . And God said to Noah, "I have determined to make an end of all flesh; for the earth is filled with violence through them; behold, I will destroy them with the earth. Make yourself an ark of gopher wood; . . . For behold, I will bring a flood of waters upon the earth, to destroy all flesh in which is the breath of life from under heaven; everything that is on the earth shall die. But I will establish my covenant with you; and you shall come into the ark, you, your sons, your wife, and your sons' wives with you. . . . Noah did this; he did all that God commanded him.

Then the Lord said to Noah, "Go into the ark, you and all your household, for I have seen that you are righteous before me in this generation. Take with you seven pairs of all clean animals, the male and his mate; and a pair of the animals that are not clean, the male and his mate; and seven pairs of the birds of the air also, male and female, to keep their kind alive upon the face of all the earth. For in seven days I will send rain upon the earth forty days and forty nights; and every living thing that I have made

I will blot out from the face of the ground." And Noah did all that the Lord had commanded him.

The flood continued forty days upon the earth; and the waters increased, and bore up the ark, and it rose high above the earth.

But God remembered Noah and all the beasts and all the cattle that were with him in the ark. And God made a wind blow over the earth, and the waters subsided. . . . [Noah] waited another seven days, and again he sent forth the dove out of the ark; and the dove came back to him in the evening, and behold, in her mouth a freshly plucked olive leaf; so Noah knew that the waters had subsided from the earth. . . . Then Noah built an altar to the Lord, and took of every clean animal and of every clean bird, and offered burnt offerings on the altar.

And God said, "This is the sign of the covenant which I make between me and you and every living creature that is with you, for all future generations: I set my bow in the cloud, and it shall be a sign of the covenant between me and the earth.

TODAY WE SEE A DOVE AND A RAINBOW AND WE READ THE STORY OF NOAH'S ARK. The sins of mankind had multiplied until the hearts of the people were "only evil continually" (Gen 6:5). Jewish tradition tells us that pride and wickedness and violence were so common in this time that humanity would have destroyed itself completely. We read that God wished to cleanse the earth and allow humanity to begin again. The story of the flood helps us to understand the gravity of sin and God's desire for our redemption.

After the waters of the flood began to subside, Noah sent out a dove, and it returned carrying a green olive branch, which showed that the land was again dry and safe. God set a rainbow in the sky as a symbol of his promise to Noah and all creatures to never again flood the earth. The flood waters are a symbol to us of our own baptisms, in which we are washed clean of sin and given "a new beginning of goodness."

O God, we thank you for your mercy and your justice, and for the new beginning of Baptism. Help us to forgive and to ask for forgiveness. AMEN.

THE PROMISE

GENESIS 12:1–7, 15:1–6

Now the Lord said to Abram, "Go from your country and your kindred and your father's house to the land that I will show you. And I will make of you a great nation, and I will bless you, and make your name great, so that you will be a blessing. I will bless those who bless you, and him who curses you I will curse; and by you all the families of the earth shall bless themselves."

So Abram went, as the Lord had told him; and Lot went with him. Abram was seventy-five years old when he departed from Haran. And Abram took Sarai his wife, and Lot his brother's son, and all their possessions . . . and they set forth to go to the land of Canaan. When they had come to the land of Canaan, Abram passed through the land to the place at Shechem, to the oak of Moreh. At that time the Canaanites were in the land. Then the Lord appeared to Abram, and said, "To your descendants I will give this land." So he built there an altar to the Lord, who had appeared to him.

After these things the word of the Lord came to Abram in a vision, "Fear not, Abram, I am your shield; your reward shall be very great." But Abram

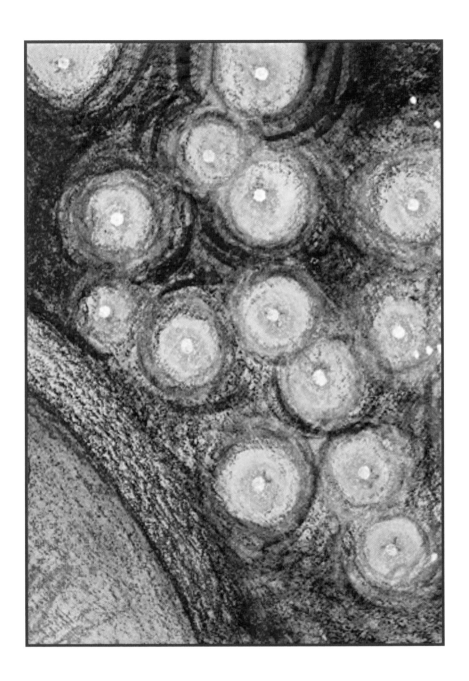

said, "O Lord God, what will you give me, for I continue childless, and the heir of my house is Eliezer of Damascus?" And Abram said, "Behold, you have given me no offspring; and a slave born in my house will be my heir." And behold, the word of the Lord came to him, "This man shall not be your heir; your own son shall be your heir." And he brought him outside and said, "Look toward heaven, and number the stars, if you are able to number them." Then he said to him, "So shall your descendants be." And he believed the Lord; and he reckoned it to him as righteousness.

TODAY WE SEE A FIELD OF STARS AND WE READ ABOUT GOD'S PROMISE TO ABRAHAM (who at this point is still Abram, before God gives him and his wife Sarai/Sarah new names). In the tenth generation after Noah, Abraham is born. God promised that he would make of Abraham "a great nation" (Gen 12:2) and that his descendants would be as numerous as the stars in the heavens (Gen 15:5).

That he would become a great nation came as a surprise to Abraham as he packed up his household at God's request and left his home to settle in a for-

eign land. That he would have many descendants was hard to believe, because he and his wife were already old, and they had no children. But he did believe. He accepted God's plan for his life. He accepted that God's promises to him would be fulfilled. For this reason we call Abraham "our father in faith."

O God, as we prepare for Christmas, we recall the way that Mary also accepted that God's promises to her would be fulfilled. Help us know and accept your will in our lives. AMEN.

THE OFFERING OF ISAAC

GENESIS 22:1-14

After these things God tested Abraham, and said to him, "Abraham!" And he said, "Here am I." He said, "Take your son, your only-begotten son Isaac, whom you love, and go to the land of Moriah, and offer him there as a burnt offering upon one of the mountains of which I shall tell you."

So Abraham rose early in the morning, saddled his donkey, and took two of his young men with him, and his son Isaac; and he cut the wood for the burnt offering, and arose and went to the place of which God had told him. On the third day Abraham lifted up his eyes and saw the place afar off. Then Abraham said to his young men, "Stay here with the donkey; I and the lad will go yonder and worship, and come again to you." And Abraham took the wood of the burnt offering, and laid it on Isaac his son; and he took in his hand the fire and the knife. So they went both of them together. And Isaac said to his father Abraham, "My father!" And he said, "Here am I, my son." He said, "Behold, the fire and the wood; but where is the lamb for a burnt offering?" Abraham said, "God will provide

himself the lamb for a burnt offering, my son." So they went both of them together.

When they came to the place of which God had told him, Abraham built an altar there, and laid the wood in order, and bound Isaac his son, and laid him on the altar, upon the wood. Then Abraham put forth his hand, and took the knife to slay his son. But the angel of the Lord called to him from heaven, and said, "Abraham, Abraham!" And he said, "Here am I." He said, "Do not lay your hand on the lad or do anything to him; for now I know that you fear God, seeing you have not withheld your son, your only-begotten son, from me." And Abraham lifted up his eyes and looked, and behold, behind him was a ram, caught in a thicket by his horns; and Abraham went and took the ram, and offered it up as a burnt offering instead of his son. So Abraham called the name of that place The Lord will provide; as it is said to this day, "On the mount of the Lord it shall be provided."

TODAY WE SEE A RAM AND WE READ THE STORY OF GOD'S TEST OF ABRAHAM. God instructed Abraham to offer his son Isaac as a sacrifice. This test is not easy for us to understand. But God had promised Abraham that he would

have descendants through Isaac. So Abraham's willingness to sacrifice his beloved son shows that he trusted that somehow Isaac would live. Saint Paul tells us, "He considered that God was able to raise men even from the dead" (Heb 11:19). When God saw that Abraham's faith had passed the test, he stayed Abraham's hand and instead provided for them a ram for their sacrifice.

Nearly two thousand years later, God himself, in his great love for humanity, offered his own beloved Son as a sacrifice. Isaac, who carried the wood for his sacrifice up the mountain, reminds us of Jesus, who carried the wooden cross up the mountain at Golgotha.

O God, help us to give you our whole hearts, not reserving any part of our lives from you. Help us to grow in faith and trust and to love you more and more. AMEN.

ASSURANCE OF THE PROMISE

GENESIS 27:41–44, 28:10–17

Now Esau hated Jacob because of the blessing with which his father had blessed him, and Esau said to himself, "The days of mourning for my father are approaching; then I will kill my brother Jacob." But the words of Esau her older son were told to Rebekah; so she sent and called Jacob her younger son, and said to him, "Behold, your brother Esau comforts himself by planning to kill you. Now therefore, my son, obey my voice; arise, flee to Laban my brother in Haran, and stay with him a while, until your brother's fury turns away. . . .

Jacob left Beer-sheba, and went toward Haran. And he came to a certain place, and stayed there that night, because the sun had set. Taking one of the stones of the place, he put it under his head and lay down in that place to sleep. And he dreamed that there was a ladder set up on the earth, and the top of it reached to heaven; and behold, the angels of God were ascending and descending on it! And behold, the Lord stood above it and said, "I am the Lord, the God of Abraham your father and the God of Isaac; the land on which you lie I will give to you and to

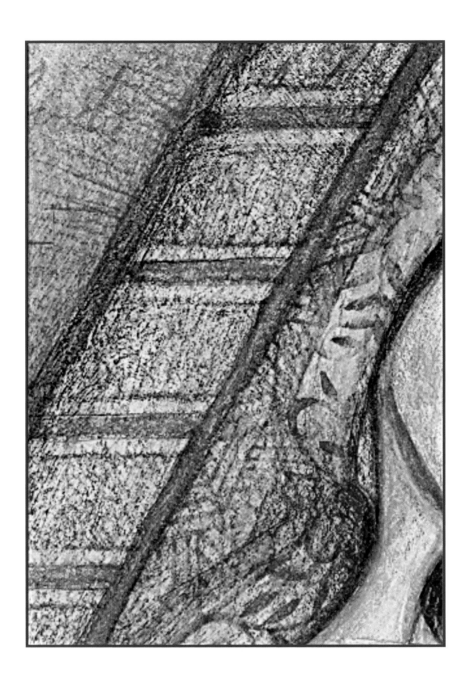

your descendants; and your descendants shall be like the dust of the earth, and you shall spread abroad to the west and to the east and to the north and to the south; and by you and your descendants shall all the families of the earth bless themselves. Behold, I am with you and will keep you wherever you go, and will bring you back to this land; for I will not leave you until I have done that of which I have spoken to you." Then Jacob awoke from his sleep and said, "Surely the Lord is in this place; and I did not know it." And he was afraid, and said, "How awesome is this place! This is none other than the house of God, and this is the gate of heaven."

TODAY WE SEE A LADDER AND WE READ THE STORY OF JACOB'S MESSAGE FROM GOD. Jacob was fleeing from the wrath of his brother when he was visited by God in a dream. He saw a ladder upon which angels were traveling between heaven and earth. God assured Jacob that the promises he had made to Jacob's father Isaac and his grandfather Abraham would be fulfilled in him. Jacob awoke and praised God.

Jacob's ladder reminds us of the very real connection between heaven and earth. Angels bring messages

down from God. Our prayers ascend to heaven. Our work to overcome our defects and grow in personal holiness throughout our lives can be seen as an ascent of this ladder, one rung at a time, towards heaven. The ladder itself can be seen as a symbol of Jesus, through whom we can reach heaven.

O God, we know that you have a plan for each of us. During this season of Advent, help us to trust you more, to pray more, to know our defects, and to work to overcome them. AMEN.

GOD'S PROVIDENCE

GENESIS 37:3–8, 12, 17–28

Now Israel loved Joseph more than any other of his children, because he was the son of his old age; and he made him a long robe with sleeves. But when his brothers saw that their father loved him more than all his brothers, they hated him, and could not speak peaceably to him.

Now Joseph had a dream, and when he told it to his brothers they only hated him the more. He said to them, "Hear this dream which I have dreamed: behold, we were binding sheaves in the field, and behold, my sheaf arose and stood upright; and behold, your sheaves gathered round it, and bowed down to my sheaf." His brothers said to him, "Are you indeed to reign over us? Or are you indeed to have dominion over us?" So they hated him yet more for his dreams and for his words. . . .

Now his brothers went to pasture their father's flock near Shechem. . . . So Joseph went after his brothers, and found them at Dothan. They saw him afar off, and before he came near to them they conspired against him to kill him. They said to one another, "Here comes this dreamer. Come now, let us kill him and throw him into one of the pits; then we

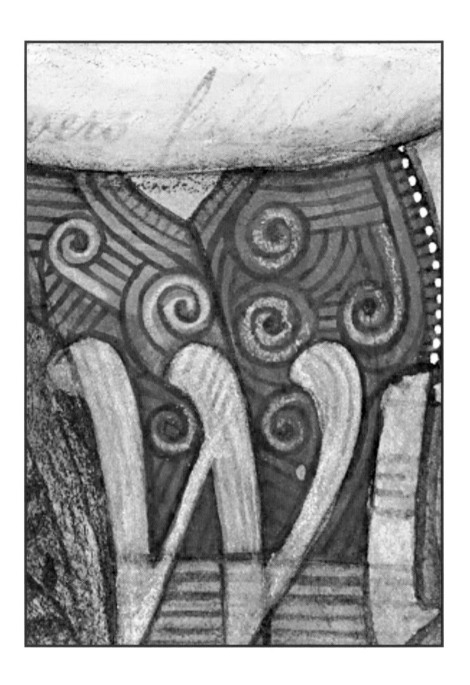

shall say that a wild beast has devoured him, and we shall see what will become of his dreams." But when Reuben heard it, he delivered him out of their hands, saying, "Let us not take his life." And Reuben said to them, "Shed no blood; cast him into this pit here in the wilderness, but lay no hand upon him"—that he might rescue him out of their hand, to restore him to his father. So when Joseph came to his brothers, they stripped him of his robe, the long robe with sleeves that he wore; and they took him and cast him into a pit. The pit was empty, there was no water in it.

Then they sat down to eat; and looking up they saw a caravan of Ishmaelites coming from Gilead, with their camels bearing gum, balm, and myrrh, on their way to carry it down to Egypt. Then Judah said to his brothers, "What profit is it if we slay our brother and conceal his blood? Come, let us sell him to the Ishmaelites, and let not our hand be upon him, for he is our brother, our own flesh." And his brothers heeded him. Then Midianite traders passed by; and they drew Joseph up and lifted him out of the pit, and sold him to the Ishmaelites for twenty shekels of silver; and they took Joseph to Egypt.

TODAY WE SEE JOSEPH'S COAT AND READ HIS AMAZING STORY. Joseph was sold into slavery by his older brothers, who were annoyed that he was their father's favorite (and also rather a know-it-all). Later, he was thrown into prison for a crime he didn't commit. But he did not despair. At each setback Joseph trusted God and began again. Eventually he was raised by the pharaoh himself to the position of second-in-command of all of Egypt. He was in charge of the resources of Egypt during years of plenty and of famine, and was able to save his family back home from starvation.

God did not will the sinful actions of Joseph's brothers, but through his providence, he was able to turn those actions to good. Joseph's gift of interpretation of dreams, which had been the source of the rift with his brothers, eventually led to their reunification and reconciliation.

O God, thank you for the blessing of family. Help us to share the particular talents you have given to each of us with gentleness and humility, and to see and admire you in the talents you have given to others. AMEN.

GOD'S LEADERSHIP

EXODUS 3:1-15

Now Moses was keeping the flock of his father-in-law, Jethro, the priest of Midian; and he led his flock to the west side of the wilderness, and came to Horeb, the mountain of God. And the angel of the Lord appeared to him in a flame of fire out of the midst of a bush; and he looked, and behold, the bush was burning, yet it was not consumed. And Moses said, "I will turn aside and see this great sight, why the bush is not burnt." When the Lord saw that he turned aside to see, God called to him out of the bush, "Moses, Moses!" And he said, "Here am I." Then he said, "Do not come near; put off your shoes from your feet, for the place on which you are standing is holy ground." And he said, "I am the God of your father, the God of Abraham, the God of Isaac, and the God of Jacob." And Moses hid his face, for he was afraid to look at God.

Then the Lord said, "I have seen the affliction of my people who are in Egypt, and have heard their cry because of their taskmasters; I know their sufferings, and I have come down to deliver them out of the hand of the Egyptians, and to bring them up out of that land to a good and broad land, a land flowing with milk and honey, to the place

of the Canaanites, the Hittites, the Amorites, the Perizzites, the Hivites, and the Jebusites. And now, behold, the cry of the sons of Israel has come to me, and I have seen the oppression with which the Egyptians oppress them. Come, I will send you to Pharaoh that you may bring forth my people, the sons of Israel, out of Egypt." But Moses said to God, "Who am I that I should go to Pharaoh, and bring the sons of Israel out of Egypt?" He said, "But I will be with you; and this shall be the sign for you, that I have sent you: when you have brought forth the people out of Egypt, you shall serve God upon this mountain."

Then Moses said to God, "If I come to the sons of Israel and say to them, 'The God of your fathers has sent me to you,' and they ask me, 'What is his name?' what shall I say to them?" God said to Moses, "I am who I am." And he said, "Say this to the sons of Israel, 'I am has sent me to you.'" God also said to Moses, "Say this to the sons of Israel, 'The Lord, the God of your fathers, the God of Abraham, the God of Isaac, and the God of Jacob, has sent me to you': this is my name for ever, and thus I am to be remembered throughout all generations.

TODAY WE SEE THE FLAME OF THE BURN-
ING BUSH AND WE READ THE STORY OF
MOSES' ENCOUNTER WITH GOD IN THE
DESERT. From the flames of the bush, burning
but not consumed, God's voice commanded Moses
to become a great prophet and the deliverer of the
Israelites from their slavery in Egypt. Moses was
surprised by God's confidence in him. He wasn't
powerful, or charismatic, or eloquent. But to each
objection Moses made, God reminded him, "I will
be with you" (Exod 3:12).

God loves to make use of unlikely helpers, as we see
in the stories of the Bible, and the lives of the saints,
and even in the Virgin Mary, chosen by God to be
the mother of Jesus. Early Church Fathers recognized in the burning bush a beautiful Advent symbol. Just as the burning bush was on fire without
being consumed, the Virgin Mary gave birth to the
baby Jesus while remaining a virgin.

O God, thank you for the grace available
to us in difficult times. Help us to
recognize that you are always with us, and that in
you all things are possible. AMEN.

PASSOVER

EXODUS 13:3-16

And Moses said to the people, "Remember this day, in which you came out from Egypt, out of the house of bondage, for by strength of hand the Lord brought you out from this place; no leavened bread shall be eaten. This day you are to go forth, in the month of Abib. And when the Lord brings you into the land of the Canaanites, the Hittites, the Amorites, the Hivites, and the Jebusites, which he swore to your fathers to give you, a land flowing with milk and honey, you shall keep this service in this month. Seven days you shall eat unleavened bread, and on the seventh day there shall be a feast to the Lord. Unleavened bread shall be eaten for seven days; no leavened bread shall be seen with you, and no leaven shall be seen with you in all your territory. And you shall tell your son on that day, 'It is because of what the Lord did for me when I came out of Egypt.' And it shall be to you as a sign on your hand and as a memorial between your eyes, that the law of the Lord may be in your mouth; for with a strong hand the Lord has brought you out of Egypt. You shall therefore keep this ordinance at its appointed time from year to year.

"And when the Lord brings you into the land of the Canaanites, as he swore to you and your fathers, and shall give it to you, you shall set apart to the Lord all that first opens the womb. All the firstlings of your cattle that are males shall be the Lord's. Every firstling of a donkey you shall redeem with a lamb, or if you will not redeem it you shall break its neck. Every first-born of man among your sons you shall redeem. And when in time to come your son asks you, 'What does this mean?' you shall say to him, 'By strength of hand the Lord brought us out of Egypt, from the house of bondage. For when Pharaoh stubbornly refused to let us go, the Lord slew all the first-born in the land of Egypt, both the first-born of man and the first-born of cattle. Therefore I sacrifice to the Lord all the males that first open the womb; but all the first-born of my sons I redeem.' It shall be as a mark on your hand or frontlets between your eyes; for by a strong hand the Lord brought us out of Egypt."

TODAY, WE SEE A LAMB AND WE READ THE EXPLANATION OF HOW AND WHY THE PASSOVER IS OBSERVED. This tradition had been practiced for well over a thousand years in

Jesus' time, and is still observed by Jewish people today, two thousand years later.

We are familiar with the story of the Last Supper on Holy Thursday, when Jesus and his disciples gathered together to share the Passover meal before his passion, death, and resurrection.

At the original Passover, each family sacrificed a lamb, marked their doorposts with its blood, and roasted and consumed it. By this act of faith, the firstborn children of the Israelites were spared during the tenth plague, and they were delivered from their slavery in Egypt. In the fullness of the New Testament, we believe that Jesus himself is the true Lamb of God. At his crucifixion, he was sacrificed to save us from eternal death, and from the slavery of sin. We consume the Body of Christ in the celebration of the Eucharist, the true supper of the Lamb.

O Jesus, thank you for your example of obedience and sacrifice. Help us to love you more and strive to receive you worthily in the Eucharist. AMEN.

GIVING THE TORAH AT SINAI

EXODUS 20:1–20

And God spoke all these words, saying,
"I am the Lord your God, who brought you out of the land of Egypt, out of the house of bondage.

"You shall have no other gods before me.

"You shall not make for yourself a graven image, or any likeness of anything that is in heaven above, or that is in the earth beneath, or that is in the water under the earth; you shall not bow down to them or serve them; for I the Lord your God am a jealous God, visiting the iniquity of the fathers upon the children to the third and the fourth generation of those who hate me, but showing mercy to thousands of those who love me and keep my commandments.

"You shall not take the name of the Lord your God in vain; for the Lord will not hold him guiltless who takes his name in vain.

"Remember the sabbath day, to keep it holy. Six days you shall labor, and do all your work; but the

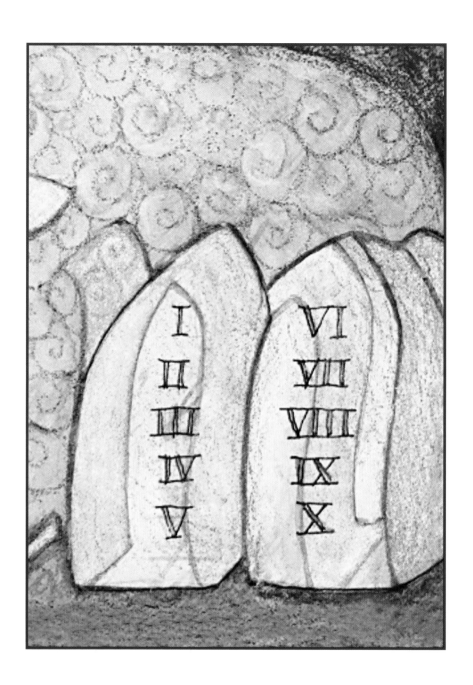

seventh day is a sabbath to the Lord your God; in it you shall not do any work, you, or your son, or your daughter, your manservant, or your maidservant, or your cattle, or the sojourner who is within your gates; for in six days the Lord made heaven and earth, the sea, and all that is in them, and rested the seventh day; therefore the Lord blessed the sabbath day and hallowed it.

"Honor your father and your mother, that your days may be long in the land which the Lord your God gives you.

"You shall not kill.

"You shall not commit adultery.

"You shall not steal.

"You shall not bear false witness against your neighbor.

"You shall not covet your neighbor's house; you shall not covet your neighbor's wife, or his manservant, or his maidservant, or his ox, or his donkey, or anything that is your neighbor's."

Now when all the people perceived the thunder

and the lightning and the sound of the trumpet and the mountain smoking, the people were afraid and trembled; and they stood afar off, and said to Moses, "You speak to us, and we will hear; but let not God speak to us, lest we die." And Moses said to the people, "Do not fear; for God has come to test you, and that the fear of him may be before your eyes, that you may not sin."

TODAY WE SEE THE TABLETS OF THE TEN COMMANDMENTS AND WE READ THE STORY OF THEIR REVELATION TO MOSES. The Torah, also known as the Pentateuch, is the first five books of the Hebrew Bible. These books contain history, stories, and laws of the Israelites from creation through the death of Moses. Christianity values the Torah, and its ability to help us understand important truths about God, ourselves, and the world.

The laws enumerated in the Pentateuch have been fulfilled and perfected in Jesus Christ, who is the New Covenant. Because of this, Christians are not bound to observe them as a religious practice. However, many of these laws, notably the Ten Commandments, are considered to be both

revealed law and natural law. They promote a way of worshipping God and treating each other that is written on our hearts and can be recognized by our reason. This is why we obey them still.

O God, thank you for your laws, given to Moses and written on our hearts. Help us to love you and our neighbor by keeping your commandments. AMEN.

THE FALL OF JERICHO

JOSHUA 6:1-7, 12-20

Now Jericho was shut up from within and from without because of the sons of Israel; none went out, and none came in. And the Lord said to Joshua, "See, I have given into your hand Jericho, with its king and mighty men of valor. You shall march around the city, all the men of war going around the city once. Thus shall you do for six days. And seven priests shall bear seven trumpets of rams' horns before the ark; and on the seventh day you shall march around the city seven times, the priests blowing the trumpets. And when they make a long blast with the ram's horn, as soon as you hear the sound of the trumpet, then all the people shall shout with a great shout; and the wall of the city will fall down flat, and the people shall go up every man straight before him." So Joshua the son of Nun called the priests and said to them, "Take up the ark of the covenant, and let seven priests bear seven trumpets of rams' horns before the ark of the Lord." And he said to the people, "Go forward; march around the city, and let the armed men pass on before the ark of the Lord."

Then Joshua rose early in the morning, and the priests took up the ark of the Lord. And the seven priests bearing the seven trumpets of rams' horns before the ark of the Lord passed on, blowing the trumpets continually; and the armed men went before them, and the rear guard came after the ark of the Lord, while the trumpets blew continually. And the second day they marched around the city once, and returned into the camp. So they did for six days.

On the seventh day they rose early at the dawn of day, and marched around the city in the same manner seven times: it was only on that day that they marched around the city seven times. And at the seventh time, when the priests had blown the trumpets, Joshua said to the people, "Shout; for the Lord has given you the city. And the city and all that is within it shall be devoted to the Lord for destruction; only Rahab the harlot and all who are with her in her house shall live, because she hid the messengers that we sent. But you, keep yourselves from the things devoted to destruction, lest when you have devoted them you take any of the devoted things and make the camp of Israel a thing for destruction, and bring trouble upon it. But all silver and gold, and vessels of bronze and iron, are sacred to the Lord; they shall go into the treasury of the Lord." So the people shouted, and the trumpets

were blown. As soon as the people heard the sound of the trumpet, the people raised a great shout, and the wall fell down flat, so that the people went up into the city, every man straight before him, and they took the city.

TODAY WE SEE A RAM'S HORN TRUMPET AND WE READ THE STORY OF THE CONQUEST OF THE CITY OF JERICHO. After wandering in the desert for forty years, Moses died. He had chosen the great warrior Joshua to succeed him and lead the Israelites into the Promised Land. Joshua took with him the Ark of the Covenant, an ornate gold-plated chest built to specifications given by God which housed the two stone tablets of the Ten Commandments, manna from the desert, and the flowering rod of the priest Aaron. Marching with it around the exterior walls, Joshua and his men captured the city of Jericho with trumpets and shouting.

The Ark of the Covenant carried within it the Word of God on stone. Saint John tells us that Jesus is the Word made flesh (John 1:14). The Church Fathers called Mary the Ark of the New Covenant, because she carried Jesus within her womb.

O God, you made the walls of Jericho fall at the blast of seven trumpets. Break down the walls that separate us from you and from the people around us. AMEN.

·UNLIKELY ·HEROES

JUDGES 7:2–7, 16, 19–23

The Lord said to Gideon, "The people with you are too many for me to give the Midianites into their hand, lest Israel vaunt themselves against me, saying, 'My own hand has delivered me.' Now therefore proclaim in the ears of the people, saying, 'Whoever is fearful and trembling, let him return home.'" And Gideon tested them; twenty-two thousand returned, and ten thousand remained.

And the Lord said to Gideon, "The people are still too many; take them down to the water and I will test them for you there; and he of whom I say to you, 'This man shall go with you,' shall go with you; and any of whom I say to you, 'This man shall not go with you,' shall not go." So he brought the people down to the water; and the Lord said to Gideon, "Every one that laps the water with his tongue, as a dog laps, you shall set by himself; likewise every one that kneels down to drink." And the number of those that lapped, putting their hands to their mouths, was three hundred men; but all the rest of the people knelt down to drink water. And the Lord said to Gideon, "With the three hundred men that lapped I will deliver you, and give the Midianites into your hand; and let all the others go every man to his home." . . .

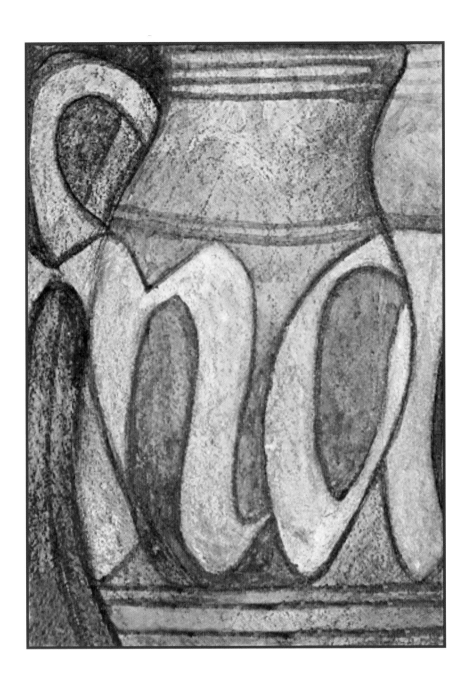

[Gideon] divided the three hundred men into three companies, and put trumpets into the hands of all of them and empty jars, with torches inside the jars. . . .

So Gideon and the hundred men who were with him came to the outskirts of the camp at the beginning of the middle watch, when they had just set the watch; and they blew the trumpets and smashed the jars that were in their hands. And the three companies blew the trumpets and broke the jars, holding in their left hands the torches, and in their right hands the trumpets to blow; and they cried, "A sword for the Lord and for Gideon!" They stood every man in his place round about the camp, and all the army ran; they cried out and fled. When they blew the three hundred trumpets, the Lord set every man's sword against his fellow and against all the army; and the army fled as far as Beth-shittah toward Zererah, as far as the border of Abel-meholah, by Tabbath. And the men of Israel were called out from Naphtali and from Asher and from all Manasseh, and they pursued after Midian.

TODAY WE SEE A CLAY JAR AND READ THE STORY OF AN OUTNUMBERED FORCE AND THEIR VICTORY IN BATTLE. It's an unlikely

story of unlikely heroes. Gideon succeeded Joshua as judge—meaning warrior-leader—of the Israelites. Many Israelites had turned their backs on God in favor of idols, and then returned to him with repentance to implore his assistance. Gideon was in command of 32,000 troops in a war with neighboring tribes. But God didn't want the Israelites to credit themselves with victory, so he had Gideon winnow down their numbers through various trials, including whether they lapped or knelt to drink water, until there were only 300 of them to fight a much larger army.

The small army brought with them trumpets and torches hidden in jars. In a confusion of trumpeting and jar-breaking, the Israelites defeated their enemies and set them to flight. Although Gideon was a flawed leader, and the Israelites continued to struggle in their faith, God was glorified through them.

O God, we know that you love us despite our weaknesses. Help us to use our lives and the gifts you have given us to glorify you. AMEN.

THE BEGINNING OF THE KINGDOM

1 SAMUEL 12:1–5, 19–24

And Samuel said to all Israel, "Behold, I have listened to your voice in all that you have said to me, and have made a king over you. And now, behold, the king walks before you; and I am old and gray, and behold, my sons are with you; and I have walked before you from my youth until this day. Here I am; testify against me before the Lord and before his anointed. Whose ox have I taken? Or whose donkey have I taken? Or whom have I defrauded? Whom have I oppressed? Or from whose hand have I taken a bribe to blind my eyes with it? Testify against me and I will restore it to you." They said, "You have not defrauded us or oppressed us or taken anything from any man's hand." And he said to them, "The Lord is witness against you, and his anointed is witness this day, that you have not found anything in my hand." And they said, "He is witness."

. . . And all the people said to Samuel, "Pray for your servants to the Lord your God, that we may not die; for we have added to all our sins this evil, to ask for ourselves a king." And Samuel said to the people, "Fear not; you have done all this evil,

yet do not turn aside from following the Lord, but serve the Lord with all your heart; and do not turn aside after vain things which cannot profit or save, for they are vain. For the Lord will not cast away his people, for his great name's sake, because it has pleased the Lord to make you a people for himself. Moreover as for me, far be it from me that I should sin against the Lord by ceasing to pray for you; and I will instruct you in the good and the right way. Only fear the Lord, and serve him faithfully with all your heart; for consider what great things he has done for you.

TODAY WE SEE A CROWN AND WE READ THE FAREWELL ADDRESS OF THE PROPHET SAMUEL. Samuel reluctantly ushered in the era of kings of Israel. The Israelites were historically ruled directly by God, under the leadership of the judges and prophets. But after a string of poor leaders, the Israelites decided they'd rather be "like all the nations" (1 Sam 8:20) and have a king. Monarchy as a form of government isn't wrong in itself, but it was wrong for the people of Israel to seek to distance themselves from God. Samuel tried to warn them, but they wouldn't hear it, so he anointed Saul as their king. The people

soon came to regret their demands and lament Saul's kingship.

This is understandable, as Saul was a very disturbed man. But human leadership will almost always disappoint us. This is why, above any national government, we recognize Jesus Christ as our king and the King of the Universe.

O God, you are the king and ruler of all nations. Protect our family, our country, and our Church from all dangers within and without. Help us to acknowledge you as king of our hearts. AMEN.

A SHEPHERD FOR THE PEOPLE

2 SAMUEL 5:1–3; 7:1–5, 8–9,11B–14A

Then all the tribes of Israel came to David at Hebron, and said, "Behold, we are your bone and flesh. In times past, when Saul was king over us, it was you that led out and brought in Israel; and the Lord said to you, 'You shall be shepherd of my people Israel, and you shall be prince over Israel.'" So all the elders of Israel came to the king at Hebron; and King David made a covenant with them at Hebron before the Lord, and they anointed David king over Israel. . . .

Now when the king dwelt in his house, and the Lord had given him rest from all his enemies round about, the king said to Nathan the prophet, "See now, I dwell in a house of cedar, but the ark of God dwells in a tent." And Nathan said to the king, "Go, do all that is in your heart; for the Lord is with you."

But that same night the word of the Lord came to Nathan, "Go and tell my servant David, 'Thus says the Lord: Would you build me a house to dwell in? . . . Now therefore thus you shall say to my servant

69

David, 'Thus says the Lord of hosts, I took you from the pasture, from following the sheep, that you should be prince over my people Israel; and I have been with you wherever you went, and have cut off all your enemies from before you; and I will make for you a great name, like the name of the great ones of the earth. . . . Moreover the Lord declares to you that the Lord will make you a house. When your days are fulfilled and you lie down with your fathers, I will raise up your offspring after you, who shall come forth from your body, and I will establish his kingdom. He shall build a house for my name, and I will establish the throne of his kingdom for ever. I will be his father, and he shall be my son. . . .

TODAY WE SEE THE SHEPHERD'S CROOK AND WE READ ABOUT KING DAVID. Before he was king, David was a shepherd boy. As a young man he was the head of King Saul's armies, and the occasional target of Saul's attempted murders. When Saul was killed in battle, David was chosen to be king. God promised King David: "Your house and your kingdom shall be made sure for ever before me; your throne shall be established for ever" (2 Sam 7:16).

The New Testament begins with a genealogy, to show that Jesus Christ is the fulfillment of that promise. Saint Matthew wrote that Jesus is the Messiah, "the son of David, the son of Abraham" (Matt 1:1). Jesus is the Davidic king of all peoples and over all the earth. He is also the Good Shepherd. Artistic representations of a young Jesus carrying a lamb over his shoulders can be seen in the catacombs, tombs, and baptismal fonts of the first Christians, a reminder of David, and the prophecy fulfilled.

O Jesus, you are the Good Shepherd, who gives his life for his sheep. Help us to hear and follow your voice. AMEN.

THE THREAT OF FALSE GODS

1 KINGS 18:20-39

So Ahab sent to all the sons of Israel, and gathered the prophets together at Mount Carmel. And Elijah came near to all the people, and said, "How long will you go limping with two different opinions? If the Lord is God, follow him; but if Baal, then follow him." And the people did not answer him a word. Then Elijah said to the people, "I, even I only, am left a prophet of the Lord; but Baal's prophets are four hundred and fifty men. Let two bulls be given to us; and let them choose one bull for themselves, and cut it in pieces and lay it on the wood, but put no fire to it; and I will prepare the other bull and lay it on the wood, and put no fire to it. And you call on the name of your god and I will call on the name of the Lord; and the God who answers by fire, he is God." And all the people answered, "It is well spoken." Then Elijah said to the prophets of Baal, "Choose for yourselves one bull and prepare it first, for you are many; and call on the name of your god, but put no fire to it." And they took the bull which was given them, and they prepared it, and called on the name of Baal from morning until noon, saying, "O Baal, answer us!" But there was

73

no voice, and no one answered. And they limped about the altar which they had made. And at noon Elijah mocked them, saying, "Cry aloud, for he is a god; either he is musing, or he has gone aside, or he is on a journey, or perhaps he is asleep and must be awakened." And they cried aloud, and cut themselves after their custom with swords and lances, until the blood gushed out upon them. And as midday passed, they raved on until the time of the offering of the oblation, but there was no voice; no one answered, no one heeded.

Then Elijah said to all the people, "Come near to me"; and all the people came near to him. And he repaired the altar of the Lord that had been thrown down; Elijah took twelve stones, according to the number of the tribes of the sons of Jacob, to whom the word of the Lord came, saying, "Israel shall be your name"; and with the stones he built an altar in the name of the Lord. And he made a trench about the altar, as great as would contain two measures of seed. And he put the wood in order, and cut the bull in pieces and laid it on the wood. And he said, "Fill four jars with water, and pour it on the burnt offering, and on the wood." And he said, "Do it a second time"; and they did it a second time. And he said, "Do it a third time"; and they did it a third time. And

the water ran round about the altar, and filled the trench also with water.

And at the time of the offering of the oblation, Elijah the prophet came near and said, "O Lord, God of Abraham, Isaac, and Israel, let it be known this day that you are God in Israel, and that I am your servant, and that I have done all these things at your word. Answer me, O Lord, answer me, that this people may know that you, O Lord, are God, and that you have turned their hearts back." Then the fire of the Lord fell, and consumed the burnt offering, and the wood, and the stones, and the dust, and licked up the water that was in the trench. And when all the people saw it, they fell on their faces; and they said, "The Lord, he is God; the Lord, he is God."

TODAY WE SEE A STONE ALTAR AND WE READ THE STORY OF ELIJAH'S DEFEAT OF THE PRIESTS OF A PAGAN GOD. Elijah was a prophet during the reign of the wicked Ahab, a king who turned the people of Israel to the worship of the god Baal. In a contest, the prophets of Baal were unable to call down fire to consume their sacrifice, but when Elijah prayed

to God, fire came down from heaven to consume not only the sacrifice but also the altar.

Jesus Christ is "the Priest, the Altar, and the Lamb of sacrifice." He is the priest because he makes the offering, he is the sacrifice because he offers himself, and he is the altar because his incarnate human body is the place of the sacrifice. Saint Ambrose asked, "For what is the altar of Christ if not the image of the Body of Christ?" This is why we bow in reverence to the altar if Jesus is not there present in the tabernacle.

O Jesus, you became man and offered yourself as a sacrifice for us. Help us to grow in love for you as we ponder the mystery of your incarnation. AMEN.

FAITHFULNESS AND DELIVERANCE

2 KINGS 19:14–20, 32–34

Hezekiah received the letter from the hand of the messengers, and read it; and Hezekiah went up to the house of the Lord, and spread it before the Lord. And Hezekiah prayed before the Lord, and said: "O Lord the God of Israel, who are enthroned above the cherubim, you are the God, you alone, of all the kingdoms of the earth; you have made heaven and earth. Incline your ear, O Lord, and hear; open your eyes, O Lord, and see; and hear the words of Sennacherib, which he has sent to mock the living God. Of a truth, O Lord, the kings of Assyria have laid waste the nations and their lands, and have cast their gods into the fire; for they were no gods, but the work of men's hands, wood and stone; therefore they were destroyed. So now, O Lord our God, save us, I beg you, from his hand, that all the kingdoms of the earth may know that you, O Lord, are God alone."

Then Isaiah the son of Amoz sent to Hezekiah, saying, "Thus says the Lord, the God of Israel: Your prayer to me about Sennacherib king of Assyria I have heard.

"Therefore thus says the Lord concerning the king of Assyria, He shall not come into this city or shoot an arrow there, or come before it with a shield or cast up a siege mound against it. By the way that he came, by the same he shall return, and he shall not come into this city, says the Lord. For I will defend this city to save it, for my own sake and for the sake of my servant David."

TODAY WE SEE AN EMPTY TENT AND READ THE PRAYER OF HEZEKIAH. Hezekiah was the son of Ahaz. He succeeded Ahaz as king and worked to right the misdeeds of his father. Parts of the kingdom were invaded. Hezekiah sought the advice of the prophet Isaiah and turned to God in prayer, and the enemies of the Israelites were defeated, leaving only their empty tents.

After relating the genealogy of Jesus, Saint Matthew reminds us of Isaiah's prophecy: "Behold, a virgin shall conceive and bear a son, and his name shall be Emmanuel" (Matt 1:23). In the fullness of the New Testament, we see that these words of the prophet Isaiah foretold that Jesus would be born of the Virgin Mary. More immediately, they may have also foretold the birth of Hezekiah himself, when

they were spoken by Isaiah to Ahaz (Isa 7:14). Ahaz had refused to ask the Lord for a sign. God gave him his son Hezekiah as a sign of the continuation of the line of David, whose ultimate end was Jesus.

O God, we know you hear our prayers. Help us to humbly come to you when we are in need, trusting in your aid. AMEN.

THE EXILE

JEREMIAH 9:1–11

O that my head were waters,
 and my eyes a fountain of tears,
that I might weep day and night
    for the slain of the daughter of my people!
O that I had in the desert
    a wayfarers' lodging place,
that I might leave my people
    and go away from them!
For they are all adulterers,
    a company of treacherous men.
They bend their tongue like a bow;
    falsehood and not truth has grown strong in the
land;
for they proceed from evil to evil,
    and they do not know me, says the Lord.
Let every one beware of his neighbor,
    and put no trust in any brother;
for every brother is a supplanter,
    and every neighbor goes about as a slanderer.
Every one deceives his neighbor,
    and no one speaks the truth;
they have taught their tongue to speak lies;
    they commit iniquity and are too weary to repent.
Heaping oppression upon oppression, and deceit
upon deceit,

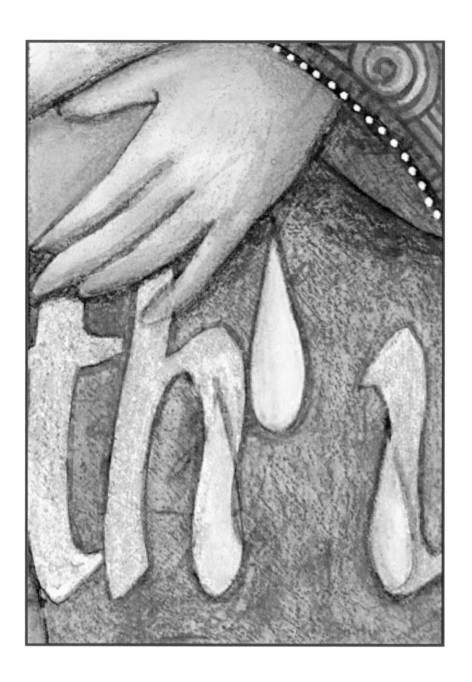

they refuse to know me, says the Lord.

Therefore thus says the Lord of hosts:
"Behold, I will refine them and test them,
    for what else can I do, because of my people?
Their tongue is a deadly arrow;
    it speaks deceitfully;
with his mouth each speaks peaceably to his
neighbor,
    but in his heart he plans an ambush for him.
Shall I not punish them for these things? says
the Lord;
    and shall I not avenge myself
    on a nation such as this?

"Take up weeping and wailing for the mountains,
    and a lamentation for the pastures of the
wilderness,
because they are laid waste so that no one passes
through,
    and the lowing of cattle is not heard;
both the birds of the air and the beasts
    have fled and are gone.
I will make Jerusalem a heap of ruins,
    a lair of jackals;
and I will make the cities of Judah a desolation,
    without inhabitant."

TODAY WE SEE THE TEARS OF JEREMIAH AND WE READ HIS SORROWFUL LAMENT. JEREMIAH WAS A PROPHET OF THE JEWISH PEOPLE DURING A HARROWING TIME. He advised stubborn and weak-willed kings, suffered the unfaithfulness of the people, witnessed the fall of Jerusalem and the destruction of Solomon's Temple, and faced exile and abuse. Throughout, he did his best to love and serve those around him and to remain true to God and his vocation, while weeping for the sins and afflictions of his community.

People in our families and our communities can still drive us to tears. We are endowed with free will and can choose sin, and ignore good advice, and turn away from God. Jeremiah knew that God would establish a new covenant with humanity. He knew that we would still need God's forgiveness. God told Jeremiah, "I will forgive their iniquity, and I will remember their sin no more" (Jer 31:34).

O Jesus, you bound yourself to us in love through the shedding of your blood. Help us to confess our sins and return to you, and to forgive those who give us cause to weep. AMEN.

WAITING

HABAKKUK 2:1–8

I will take my stand to watch,
and station myself on the tower,
and look forth to see what he will say to me,
    and what I will answer concerning my com-
plaint.
And the Lord answered me:
"Write the vision;
    make it plain upon tablets,
    so he may run who reads it.
For still the vision awaits its time;
    it hastens to the end—it will not lie.
If it seem slow, wait for it;
    it will surely come, it will not delay.
Behold, he whose soul is not upright in him shall
fail,
    but the righteous shall live by his faith.
Moreover, wine is treacherous;
    the arrogant man shall not abide.
His greed is as wide as Sheol;
    like death he has never enough.
He gathers for himself all nations,
    and collects as his own all peoples."
Shall not all these take up their taunt against him,
in scoffing derision of him, and say,

"Woe to him who heaps up what is not his own—
    for how long?—
    and loads himself with pledges!"
Will not your debtors suddenly arise,
    and those awake who will make you tremble?
    Then you will be booty for them.
Because you have plundered many nations,
    all the remnant of the peoples shall plunder you,
for the blood of men and violence to the earth,
    to cities and all who dwell therein.

TODAY WE SEE A STONE WATCHTOWER AND WE READ THE POETIC WARNINGS OF THE PROPHET HABAKKUK. Habakkuk was likely active around the same time as the prophet Jeremiah and also suffered through the distressing lead up to the Babylonian Exile. Jeremiah wept, but Habakkuk shouted. He cried out against the evils he saw, and asked God why he did not punish the evil-doers. God told Habakkuk that the unrest around him was a result of human sin and that the solution was to wait and trust in God's plans.

Waiting is never easy. But during Advent, as we wait for the coming of Christmas, we get a small taste of the very long period of expectation that preceded the

birth of Jesus. It was through the prophets that God sustained Israel's hope in the coming of the Messiah. We are waiting again, this time in hope for the second coming, when Jesus will return as universal judge.

O God, all time and all creation are yours. Give us the patience to wait in joyful hope for the salvation accomplished by Jesus Christ to be realized in its fullness. AMEN.

RETURN AND REBUILDING

NEHEMIAH 1:1B–6, 11B, 2:1–8

Now it happened in the month of Chislev, in the twentieth year, as I was in Susa the capital, that Hanani, one of my brethren, came with certain men out of Judah; and I asked them concerning the Jews that survived, who had escaped exile, and concerning Jerusalem. And they said to me, "The survivors there in the province who escaped exile are in great trouble and shame; the wall of Jerusalem is broken down, and its gates are destroyed by fire."

When I heard these words I sat down and wept, and mourned for days; and I continued fasting and praying before the God of heaven. And I said, "O Lord God of heaven, the great and terrible God who keeps covenant and merciful love with those who love him and keep his commandments; let your ear be attentive, and your eyes open, to hear the prayer of your servant which I now pray before you day and night for the people of Israel your servants, confessing the sins of the sons of Israel, which we have sinned against you. Yes, I and my father's house have sinned. . . . "

Now I was cupbearer to the king. In the month of

Nisan, in the twentieth year of King Ar-ta-xerxes, when wine was before him, I took up the wine and gave it to the king. Now I had not been sad in his presence. And the king said to me, "Why is your face sad, seeing you are not sick? This is nothing else but sadness of the heart." Then I was very much afraid. I said to the king, "Let the king live for ever! Why should not my face be sad, when the city, the place of my fathers' sepulchres, lies waste, and its gates have been destroyed by fire?" Then the king said to me, "For what do you make request?" So I prayed to the God of heaven. And I said to the king, "If it pleases the king, and if your servant has found favor in your sight, that you send me to Judah, to the city of my fathers' sepulchres, that I may rebuild it." And the king said to me (the queen sitting beside him), "How long will you be gone, and when will you return?" So it pleased the king to send me; and I set him a time. And I said to the king, "If it pleases the king, let letters be given me to the governors of the province Beyond the River, that they may let me pass through until I come to Judah; and a letter to Asaph, the keeper of the king's forest, that he may give me timber to make beams for the gates of the fortress of the temple, and for the wall of the city, and for the house which I shall occupy." And the king granted me what I asked, for the good hand of my God was upon me.

TODAY WE SEE THE WALLS OF JERUSALEM AND WE READ THE STORY OF NEHEMIAH, WHO RETURNED TO REBUILD THEM. The Babylonian Exile kept the Jewish people scattered and away from Jerusalem for about sixty years before they were allowed to return. Nehemiah was the Jewish cup-bearer of the Persian king, who allowed him to go to Jerusalem as governor and provided for him to rebuild the walls. Nehemiah rebuilt, then invited the exiles to return, and worked to restore the faith and religious practices of the Jewish community there.

Nehemiah rebuilt the outside of Jerusalem, but his efforts to renew the faith of the people were even more important. As we approach the end of the season of Advent, we prepare to decorate our homes to reflect the joy of the Christmas season. Even more importantly, we prepare our hearts to receive the news of our Savior's birth, and to renew our desire for his second coming.

O Jesus, you humbled yourself and came to us as a little child, yet Eternal God. Help us to become humble and childlike and enter more deeply into the mystery of the Incarnation. AMEN.

REPENTANCE

MATTHEW 3:1–17

In those days came John the Baptist, preaching in the wilderness of Judea, "Repent, for the kingdom of heaven is at hand." For this is he who was spoken of by the prophet Isaiah when he said,

"The voice of one crying in the wilderness:
Prepare the way of the Lord,
make his paths straight."

Now John wore a garment of camel's hair, and a leather belt around his waist; and his food was locusts and wild honey. Then went out to him Jerusalem and all Judea and all the region about the Jordan, and they were baptized by him in the river Jordan, confessing their sins.

But when he saw many of the Pharisees and Sadducees coming for baptism, he said to them, "You brood of vipers! Who warned you to flee from the wrath to come? Bear fruit that befits repentance, and do not presume to say to yourselves, 'We have Abraham as our father'; for I tell you, God is able from these stones to raise up children to Abraham. Even now the axe is laid to the root of the trees; every tree therefore that does not bear

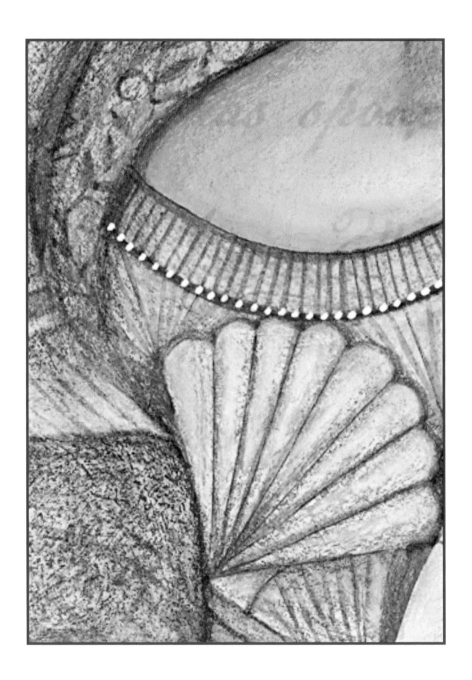

good fruit is cut down and thrown into the fire.

"I baptize you with water for repentance, but he who is coming after me is mightier than I, whose sandals I am not worthy to carry; he will baptize you with the Holy Spirit and with fire. His winnowing fork is in his hand, and he will clear his threshing floor and gather his wheat into the granary, but the chaff he will burn with unquenchable fire."

Then Jesus came from Galilee to the Jordan to John, to be baptized by him. John would have prevented him, saying, "I need to be baptized by you, and do you come to me?" But Jesus answered him, "Let it be so now; for thus it is fitting for us to fulfil all righteousness." Then he consented. And when Jesus was baptized, he went up immediately from the water, and behold, the heavens were opened and he saw the Spirit of God descending like a dove, and alighting on him; and behold, a voice from heaven, saying, "This is my beloved Son, with whom I am well pleased."

TODAY WE SEE THE SCALLOP SHELL, A SYMBOL OF BAPTISM, AND WE READ ABOUT THE MINISTRY OF SAINT JOHN THE BAPTIST. The prophets foretold that Elijah would return as a messenger to prepare the way for the Messiah. Jesus told us that Saint John the Baptist was this messenger. John baptized with a "baptism of repentance" (Mark 1:4). Jesus, of course, was sinless and had no need to repent. However, he chose to be baptized by John and so to establish the sacramental Baptism of the Church.

Sacramental Baptism in the name of the Father, and the Son, and the Holy Spirit, is a cleansing of our sins and a rebirth in Jesus Christ. In Baptism we have become "a new creation" (2 Cor 5:17). But we still sin, and so we still have need of repentance. During this season of Advent, Saint John the Baptist's call applies to each of us: "Repent, for the kingdom of heaven is at hand" (Matt 3:2).

O Jesus, you taught us the value of repentance when you asked to be baptized. Help us to recognize our sins and to seek forgiveness. AMEN.

MARY, THE HOPE FOR A FUTURE

LUKE 1:26-38

In the sixth month the angel Gabriel was sent from God to a city of Galilee named Nazareth, to a virgin betrothed to a man whose name was Joseph, of the house of David; and the virgin's name was Mary. And he came to her and said, "Hail, full of grace, the Lord is with you!" But she was greatly troubled at the saying, and considered in her mind what sort of greeting this might be. And the angel said to her, "Do not be afraid, Mary, for you have found favor with God. And behold, you will conceive in your womb and bear a son, and you shall call his name Jesus.

He will be great, and will be called the Son of the Most High;
and the Lord God will give to him the throne of his father David,
and he will reign over the house of Jacob for ever;
and of his kingdom there will be no end."

And Mary said to the angel, "How can this be, since I have no husband?" And the angel said to her,

"The Holy Spirit will come upon you,
and the power of the Most High will overshadow you;
therefore the child to be born will be called holy,
the Son of God.

And behold, your kinswoman Elizabeth in her old age has also conceived a son; and this is the sixth month with her who was called barren. For with God nothing will be impossible." And Mary said, "Behold, I am the handmaid of the Lord; let it be to me according to your word." And the angel departed from her.

TODAY WE SEE THE FACE OF THE VIRGIN MARY, AND WE READ THE STORY OF THE ANNUNCIATION. By "the Incarnation" we mean that God became flesh, assumed a human nature, and became man in the person of Jesus Christ, the second person of the Holy Trinity. It was at Christmas that the Incarnation was announced to the world. But the Word became incarnate, and was announced privately to Mary, at the Annunciation.

We see Mary as the bridge between the Old and New Testaments. From the fall of Adam and Eve,

God began to prepare mankind to be ready for the Incarnation. He made the Israelites his chosen people and through the prophets prepared them to receive the Messiah. He made a covenant with them to maintain a line of succession that ended with one young woman, from a preordained family, the House of David, a young woman specially preserved from sin. And the world held its breath and awaited her answer to the question of the angel. And she said yes.

O Virgin Mary, your "yes" changed the whole world. Thank you for your example of humility and trust. Pray for us that we may also consent to God's will in all we do. AMEN.

TRUST

MATTHEW 1:18-25

Now the birth of Jesus Christ took place in this way. When his mother Mary had been betrothed to Joseph, before they came together she was found to be with child of the Holy Spirit; and her husband Joseph, being a just man and unwilling to put her to shame, resolved to send her away quietly. But as he considered this, behold, an angel of the Lord appeared to him in a dream, saying, "Joseph, son of David, do not fear to take Mary your wife, for that which is conceived in her is of the Holy Spirit; she will bear a son, and you shall call his name Jesus, for he will save his people from their sins." All this took place to fulfil what the Lord had spoken by the prophet:

"Behold, a virgin shall conceive and bear a son, and his name shall be called Emmanuel" (which means, God with us). When Joseph woke from sleep, he did as the angel of the Lord commanded him; he took his wife, but knew her not until she had borne a son; and he called his name Jesus.

TODAY WE SEE A CARPENTER'S HAMMER AND WE READ THE STORY OF THE ANNUNCIATION TO JOSEPH. Mary was visited by Saint Gabriel the Archangel and consented to conceive by the Holy Spirit. She then shared the news of her pregnancy with her espoused husband Joseph. We read that Joseph, "resolved to send her away quietly" (Matt 1:19) from their marriage.

Some say that this is because he believed she had committed adultery. But Joseph already knew that Mary was "with child of the Holy Spirit." (Matt 1:18) As a devout Jew, Joseph was familiar with all we have seen in our journey through the Old Testament. He knew that the Messiah was expected and that Mary was of the House of David. A more likely explanation is that he thought himself unworthy to be the earthly father of the Son of God. It is for this reason that the angel in Joseph's dream reassures him, "do not fear" (Matt 1:20).

O Good Saint Joseph,

you trusted in Mary your wife, and you trusted that God had a place for you in his plan of salvation. Pray for us that we may grow in virtue. AMEN.

THE MAGI COME TO WORSHIP

MATTHEW 2:1-12

Now when Jesus was born in Bethlehem of Judea in the days of Herod the king, behold, Wise Men from the East came to Jerusalem, saying, "Where is he who has been born king of the Jews? For we have seen his star in the East, and have come to worship him." When Herod the king heard this, he was troubled, and all Jerusalem with him; and assembling all the chief priests and scribes of the people, he inquired of them where the Christ was to be born. They told him, "In Bethlehem of Judea; for so it is written by the prophet:

'And you, O Bethlehem, in the land of Judah,
are by no means least among the rulers of Judah;
for from you shall come a ruler
who will govern my people Israel.'"

Then Herod summoned the Wise Men secretly and ascertained from them what time the star appeared; and he sent them to Bethlehem, saying, "Go and search diligently for the child, and when you have found him bring me word, that I too may come and worship him." When they had heard the king

they went their way; and behold, the star which they had seen in the East went before them, till it came to rest over the place where the child was. When they saw the star, they rejoiced exceedingly with great joy; and going into the house they saw the child with Mary his mother, and they fell down and worshiped him. Then, opening their treasures, they offered him gifts, gold and frankincense and myrrh. And being warned in a dream not to return to Herod, they departed to their own country by another way.

WE SEE THE STAR OF BETHLEHEM AND WE READ THE STORY OF THE MAGI. Upon the birth of Jesus, a star rose in the sky. This might have been a natural phenomenon or it might have been a miraculous creation of God, but either way, three Magi from the East saw it. They interpreted the star as a sign of the birth of a great king, and probably assumed it meant that a son had been born to King Herod. So they set off on a journey to congratulate him. When they arrived in Jerusalem, Herod, hearing the news, "was troubled, and all Jerusalem with him" (Matt 2:3) because he worried that a powerful king had been born, not of his house.

The Magi, directed towards Bethlehem by the priests and scribes, find Jesus there with his mother, do him homage and give him gifts. The three gifts have spiritual significance: gold as a symbol of his kingship on earth, frankincense (an incense) as a symbol of his deity, and myrrh (an embalming oil) as a symbol of his death.

O Jesus, you came into the world as King, and God, and sacrifice. Help us to do you homage and give you the gift of ourselves. AMEN.

THE BIRTH OF THE MESSIAH

LUKE 2:1–20

In those days a decree went out from Caesar Augustus that all the world should be enrolled. This was the first enrollment, when Quirinius was governor of Syria. And all went to be enrolled, each to his own city. And Joseph also went up from Galilee, from the city of Nazareth, to Judea, to the city of David, which is called Bethlehem, because he was of the house and lineage of David, to be enrolled with Mary, his betrothed, who was with child. And while they were there, the time came for her to be delivered. And she gave birth to her first-born son and wrapped him in swaddling cloths, and laid him in a manger, because there was no place for them in the inn.

And in that region there were shepherds out in the field, keeping watch over their flock by night. And an angel of the Lord appeared to them, and the glory of the Lord shone around them, and they were filled with fear. And the angel said to them, "Be not afraid; for behold, I bring you good news of a great joy which will come to all the people; for to you is born this day in the city of David a Savior, who is

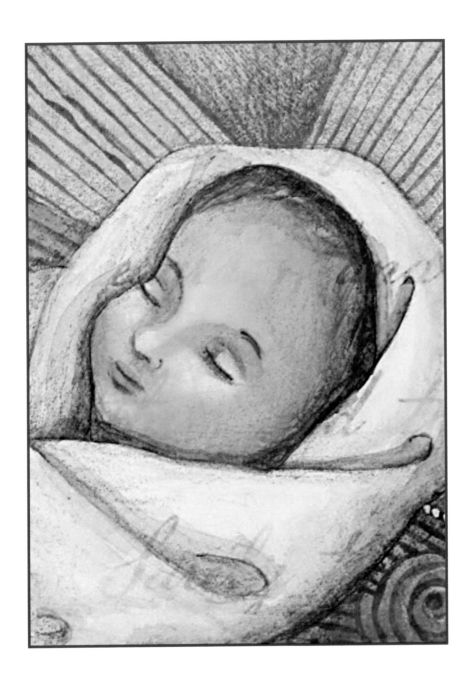

Christ the Lord. And this will be a sign for you: you will find a baby wrapped in swaddling cloths and lying in a manger." And suddenly there was with the angel a multitude of the heavenly host praising God and saying,

"Glory to God in the highest,
and on earth peace among men with whom he is pleased!"

When the angels went away from them into heaven, the shepherds said to one another, "Let us go over to Bethlehem and see this thing that has happened, which the Lord has made known to us." And they went with haste, and found Mary and Joseph, and the baby lying in a manger. And when they saw it they made known the saying which had been told them concerning this child; and all who heard it wondered at what the shepherds told them. But Mary kept all these things, pondering them in her heart. And the shepherds returned, glorifying and praising God for all they had heard and seen, as it had been told them.

CHRISTMAS IS HERE! TODAY WE SEE THE BABY JESUS AND WE READ THE STORY OF HIS HUMBLE AND TRIUMPHANT BIRTH, ATTENDED BY SHEPHERDS AND ANGELS. We rejoice with them and the whole world saying, "Glory to God in the highest!" (Luke 2:14).

Perhaps the wait of Advent seemed very long. The wait of mankind from the fall of Adam until the birth of Christ, through all the patriarchs and prophets, was a wait of thousands of years. Our Christian faith is illuminated by that wait. The Old Testament is valuable in itself as the inspired Word of God, and its fullness is revealed "in the light of Christ crucified and risen" (Catechism, no. 129). But of course, mankind is still waiting, now for Christ's second coming. We pray for Jesus' return in glory and the coming of the messianic kingdom awaited by Israel.

O Lord Jesus, you are the Word of God made flesh and born of the Virgin Mary. Thank you for coming to dwell with us on earth. We ask you to dwell always in our hearts, especially as we celebrate with joy the season of Christmas. AMEN.

MW00532110